Using The Oxford Junior Dictionary

A book of exercises and games by Philip Pullman
illustrated by Ivan Ripley

Contents

Pages 2–11   tell you about alphabetical order and show you how to look up words in a dictionary.
Pages 12–19   help you to look up words that you do not know how to spell.
Pages 20–25   explain about definitions and show you some of the things you can find out from a dictionary.
Pages 26–31   are three dictionary games.

Page	
2	**Alphabet soup**
3	**Vegetable soup**
4	**First and last**
5	**A sorting race**
6	**Talented teenager thrills tired toddlers**
7	**Two letters at a time**
8	**Library duty**
9	**Three letters at a time**
10	**If you come from . . .**
11	**Some shapes**
12	**Can you find a guilty guinea pig?**
13	**Or a gentle giraffe?**
14	**Writing about wrecks**
15	**You may need a chauffeur**
16	**Just to remind you**
17	**Words that sound the same**
18	**What do you mean—hice?**
19	**I thought you were wrong**
20	**Meanings and definitions**
21	**Which way to the balcony?**
22	**Is a crocodile a moving staircase?**
23	**Forts and fritters**
24	**Policemen, penguins and plumbers**
25	**Gunpowder, treason and plot**
26	**Spaghetti Junction**
28	**Another Maze**
30	**Round the Houses**
32	Answers

Alphabet soup

Here is the alphabet in capital letters:
ABCDEFGHIJKLMNOPQRSTUVWXYZ
And here it is in small letters:
abcdefghijklmnopqrstuvwxyz

The words in a dictionary are in alphabetical order. Alphabetical order means the order in which letters come in the alphabet.

1. Here are the first eight letters of the alphabet, all jumbled up: **GCEAHBFD**. Put them into alphabetical order.

2. Here are another eight letters: **RPTONUQS**. This time they are from the middle of the alphabet. See if you can put them into alphabetical order.

3. We can put letters into alphabetical order even when there are other letters missing between them. The letters **BDGL** are in alphabetical order. What are the missing letters?

4. Now put these letters into alphabetical order: **IMGSBJF**.

5. Here is a bowl of alphabet soup. All the letters are capitals. Try to write them down in alphabetical order.

Vegetable soup

When we want to put words into alphabetical order we have to look at the first letter of each word. Words beginning with **a** come first. Next come words beginning with **b**. After them come words beginning with **c**, and so on through the rest of the alphabet.

1. Can you put these words into alphabetical order?
   cabbage brave air elephant deceive

2. Are these words in alphabetical order?
   umbrella violin wasp xylophone yoghurt zigzag

3. This time the words start with letters from different parts of the alphabet. Put them into alphabetical order:
   monkey try boat potato funny whistle goat

4. Here are some names to put into alphabetical order:
   Nigel Karen Timothy Helen Brian Susan Jenny

5. Here is a bowl of vegetable soup with the names of the vegetables floating in it. Sort them into alphabetical order. You may find one or two words in it that are not the names of vegetables. Which are they?

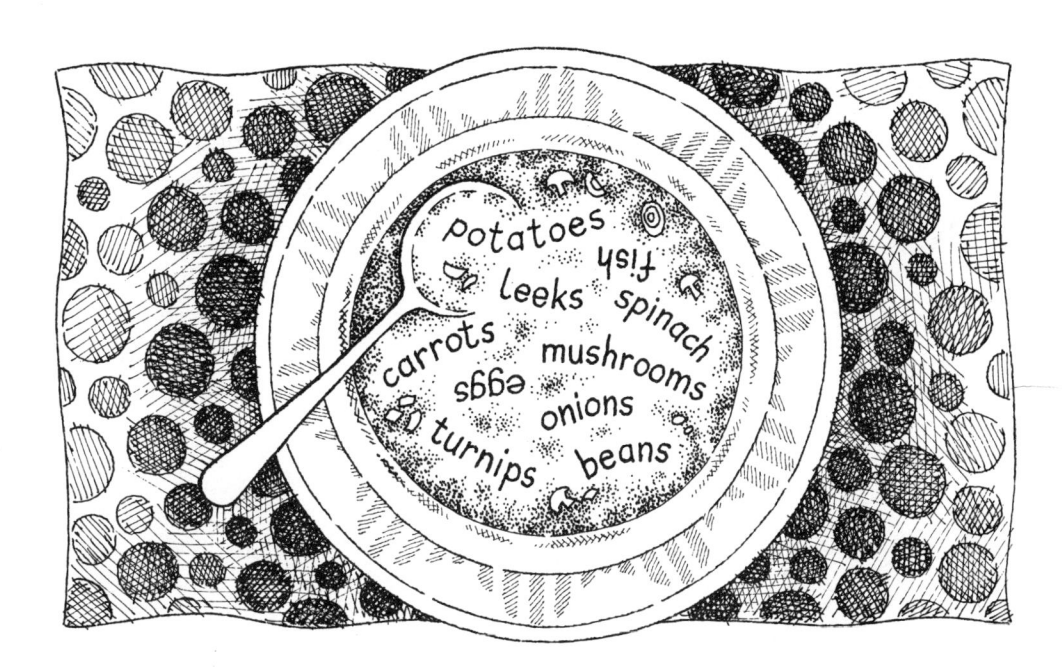

First and last

You have to look through the Dictionary carefully to find the answers to these questions.

1. What is the first word in the Dictionary beginning with **b**?
2. What is the first word in the Dictionary beginning with **c**?
3. What is the first word in the Dictionary beginning with **d**?
4. What is the first word in the Dictionary beginning with **g**?
5. What is the first word in the Dictionary beginning with **j**?
6. What is the first word in the Dictionary beginning with **k**?
7. What is the first word in the Dictionary beginning with **l**?
8. What is the first word in the Dictionary beginning with **m**?
9. What is the first word in the Dictionary beginning with **r**?
10. What is the first word in the Dictionary beginning with **t**?

For the following questions you have to look at the last word in each section of the Dictionary.

1. What is the last word in the Dictionary beginning with **a**?
2. What is the last word in the Dictionary beginning with **b**?
3. What is the last word in the Dictionary beginning with **c**?
4. What is the last word in the Dictionary beginning with **w**?
5. What is the last word in the Dictionary beginning with **j**?
6. What is the last word in the Dictionary beginning with **q**?
7. What is the last word in the Dictionary beginning with **m**?
8. What is the last word in the Dictionary beginning with **h**?
9. What is the last word in the Dictionary beginning with **l**?
10. What is the last word in the Dictionary beginning with **t**?

A sorting race

Any number can play.

Each person needs:
Twenty-six small pieces of paper
A Dictionary
Something to write with

To start with, each player writes a word on each of his pieces of paper. It does not matter what the words are, but each piece must have a different word on it, and each word must begin with a different letter of the alphabet. The dictionary will help you find some words if you cannot think of any.

When all the pieces of paper have words on them, each player shuffles his pile like a pack of cards. Then all the players start to sort their words out. The first one to get his words into alphabetical order is the winner. Next time, each player shuffles his own pile of words and gives it to the person sitting next to him to sort out.

Talented teenager thrills tired toddlers

That headline in a newspaper might be the beginning of a story about a young girl on a trapeze entertaining a group of small children. But can you see two unusual things about the words themselves?

One is that all the words begin with the letter **T**. You will find out what the other thing is when you do question 1 on this page.

When you have a number of words all beginning with the same letter and you want to put them into alphabetical order, you have to use the second letter of each word.

Here are five words beginning with **b**	bell	butter	big	bowl	baby
Their second letters are	.e..	.u....	.i.	.o..	.a..
In alphabetical order the letters are	.a..	.e..	.i.	.o..	.u....
In alphabetical order the words are	baby	bell	big	bowl	butter

1 Put these words into alphabetical order:
   thrills toddlers talented tired teenager

2 There are five children in the same class whose surnames begin with **M**. They are **Carol Muncaster, Jenny Maxwell, Gary Merton, Tony Moore** and **Alison Milton**. In what order should they go into the teacher's register?

3 You are making an index to a book you have written about ships. In what order would you put **shipwreck, submarine, sail, skipper, signal, sea**?

4 Can you make up three more headlines like 'Talented Teenager Thrills Tired Toddlers'? Use the dictionary to help you, and remember that all the words must begin with the same letter, they must be in alphabetical order, and the headline must make sense.

Two letters at a time

7

Here are six pictures of some objects. The first two letters of the name of each one are printed underneath the picture. Use the dictionary to help you find the rest of the word.

ro _ _ _ _

su _ _ _ _ _ _ _

oc _ _ _ _ _

ko _ _ _ _ _ _ _

ca _ _ _ _ _

ne _ _

Library duty

1. Jane is helping to put some books on the shelves in the school library. She has to look at the author's surname, and put the books into alphabetical order. The first five books she finds are:

   The White Tiger by Kevin Brown
   Expedition to Planet X by John Bright
   Goals! Goals! Goals! by Andrew Bryson
   Linda's Lucky Christmas by Sally Bradshaw
   The Pony Club Adventure by Caroline Brenton

   Each of the names begins with Br. But they can still be put into alphabetical order, because the **third** letter of each name is different. What order should Jane put the books in?

2. Put these words into alphabetical order:
   doodle dock doubt domino dolphin dove donkey

3. When the first **three** letters of words are the same, we have to look at the fourth letter to put them in alphabetical order. Try and sort these words out:
   decrease deceit declare decay decimal decorate

4. Here are some more names to put into order. Remember, it is the surname that you have to look at.
   Simon Crawford
   Lorraine Craven
   Karen Crane
   Andrew Craig
   Nigel Cramer
   Alison Crabbe
   David Craddock

Three letters at a time

Here are six pictures of some objects. The first three letters of the name of each one are printed underneath the picture. Use the dictionary to help you find the rest of the word.

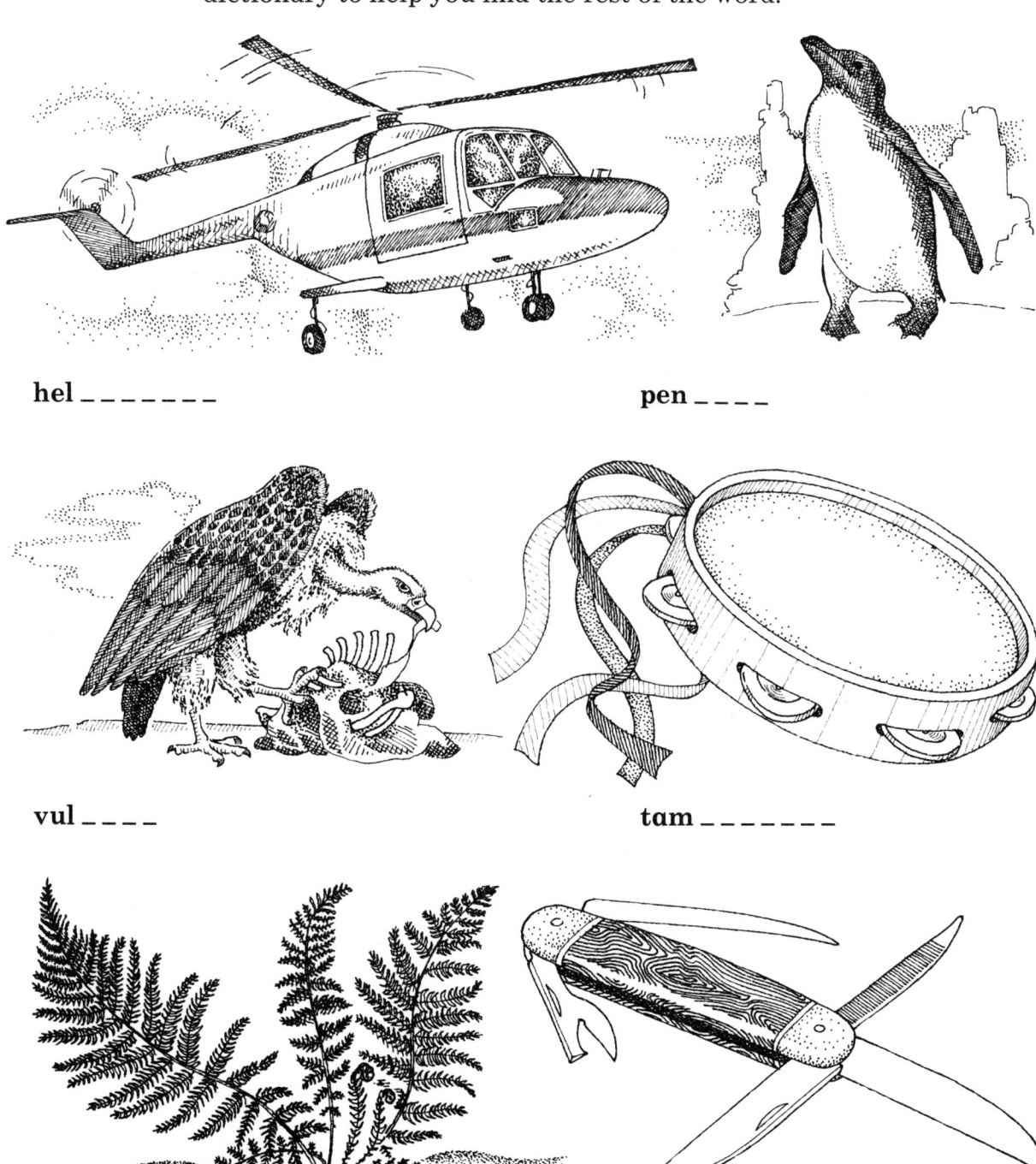

hel _ _ _ _ _ _ _

pen _ _ _ _

vul _ _ _ _

tam _ _ _ _ _ _ _

fer _

pen _ _ _ _ _

If you come from...

At the back of most dictionaries there are useful lists. On page 175 of the Oxford Junior Dictionary there are the names of a lot of different countries, with the names of the peoples who live there printed beside them. The list is in alphabetical order, so it is easy to look the words up.

Use the list to help you answer these questions:

1. What do we call people from Turkey?
2. What are people from Saudi Arabia called?
3. If you came from Spain, would you be a Spanner or a Spaniard?
4. Which people live in Holland?
5. If you come from any country in Europe, you are ──────.
6. What are people from Cyprus called?
7. People from Vietnam are called ──────.
8. What do we call people from Switzerland?
9. If you came from Greece, what would you be?
10. What are the people who come from Portugal called?
11. What do we call people from Afghanistan?
12. Which country do Lapps come from?
13. Which country do Finns come from?
14. What are people from Denmark called?
15. What are people from Burma called?

Some shapes

If you look at page 176 of the Oxford Junior Dictionary, you will find the names of a lot of different shapes. Use the pictures on that page to help you answer these questions.

1. What is the name of the flat shape that has eight sides?

2. What name do we give to the shape of a 50p piece?

3. What shape is the earth?

4. How many sides has a hexagon?

5. The flat parts that make up the sides of solid shapes are called faces. How many faces has a cube?

6. The line where two faces join is called the edge. How many edges has a cube?

7. How many faces has a cuboid?

8. What shape is a tin of baked beans?

Can you find a guilty guinea pig?

If you want to find out how to spell a word you have to guess what the first two or three letters are. Then, if you know about alphabetical order, you can look the word up in a dictionary.

But it is not easy to guess the first two or three letters of some words. For example, the word **write** sounds as if it begins with **r**. Unless you know that it begins with **wr** you would not be able to look it up in your dictionary.

Here are some ideas to help you find these difficult words.

Look up in your dictionary the words beginning with **ph**. These sound as though they begin with **f**. You may know them already, but if you do not, write down two of them and learn them. This will help to remind you of the other words that begin with **ph**.

There is one difficult word beginning with **gh**. You may know it already, but look it up to make sure.

Words beginning with **gu** are sometimes difficult so look these up too. The difficult words are those where the **u** sound is not heard. Write down and learn two of these to remind you of the words beginning with **gu**.

Now here are some sentences to correct. Write out correctly the words that have been wrongly spelt.

1 *Dad took a fotograph of the family on the beach.*
2 *Tony got an electric gitar for his birthday.*
3 *We have fizzical education lessons twice a week.*
4 *I gess the ginea pig was gilty.*
5 *Gide dogs are trained to help blind persons.*

Or a gentle giraffe?

Some words that begin with **ge** sound as though they begin with **j**. So do some words that begin with **gi**. Here are some examples:

general
generous
gentle
geography
gerbil
giant
ginger
gipsy
giraffe

Can you find any more? If you can, write them down.

There are some words that begin with **gn** but sound as though they begin with **n**. What are they? Write them down to remind you of them.

A lot of words begin with **kn** but sound as though they begin with **n**. Here are some of them:

knee   knew   knife   knit   know   knuckle

Write down some of the others to help you remember them.

Here are some more sentences to correct. Can you write down correctly the words that have been wrongly spelt?

1 *This jentle jiraffe is very fond of jingerbread.*
2 *The dog was nawing a bone in the corner.*
3 *Alison went straight up and nocked on the door.*
4 *The policeman said the letter was not jenuine. It was a forgery.*
5 *When I tried to open the drawer the nob came off in my hand.*

Writing about wrecks

Here are some more ideas to help you to look up words that you don't know how to spell.

Several words begin with **wr** but sound as though they begin with **r**. Here are some of them:
wrap
wrist
wreck
write
wriggle
wrong
Are there any others in the dictionary? If there are, write them down.

There are some words that sound as if they begin with **s** but in fact begin with **c**. These words are quite easy to remember because the next letter is always **e**, **i**, or **y**. Here are some of them:
cell
cigarette
centre
cinema
cereal
circle
Are there any words in the dictionary beginning with **cy**?

There are some words that sound as if they begin with **s** but in fact begin with **ps**. Are there any in the dictionary? If so, write them down.

Can you write these sentences out correctly?

1 *There was a huge sentipede on the salad.*
2 *My favourite sport is restling.*
3 *Sometimes I sycle to school.*
4 *I rote a sentence about a reck but it was rong.*
5 *I like sugar and milk on my sereal.*

You may need a chauffeur

There are some words that sound as if they start with a **k** but in fact start with **ch**. Here are some of them:
character
Christmas
chemist
chrome
chorus
chrysanthemum
Can you find some more?

There is another word that begins with **ch** sounding like **k**. It is **choir**. Look it up in the dictionary to see how it is said.

There are two words in the Dictionary that begin with **ch** but sound as though they begin with **sh**. They are **chalet** and **chauffeur**. They are both French words which have been taken into the English language. They are said as if they were still French. Look them up to see how they are said.

Finally, some words begin with **h** but you don't hear it when the word is said. There are not very many of these so you should be able to learn them. They are:
heir heiress honest honour hour

Here are five more sentences with some words wrongly spelt in them. Write out correctly the words that have been spelt wrongly.

1 *The school kwire sang a Kristmas hymn.*
2 *We watched the butterfly come out of its krissaliss.*
3 *Do you need a show-fur to drive you home?*
4 *The journey took five ours.*
5 *John sang the verse and the rest of us sang the korus.*

Just to remind you

The ideas on the last four pages will not answer all your spelling problems, but they may save you from looking in the wrong part of the dictionary for a word that is not there.

Here are all the ideas set out on one page so that you can find them easily:

Some words, such as	sound as though they begin with	but you should look them up in the dictionary under
photograph	f	ph
ghost	go	gh
guilt	ga, ge, gi	gu
general	j	ge
giraffe	j	gi
gnat	n	gn
knee	n	kn
write	r	wr
cell	s	ce
cigarette	s	ci
cycle	s	cy
psalm	s	ps
chemist	k	ch
chauffeur	sh	ch
heir	air	h
honest	on	h
hour	our	h

Words that sound the same

Sometimes two words sound the same but are spelt differently and have different meanings.

Here is an example:

manner means **the way something happens or is done**
manor   means **a big, important house in the country**

Here are some more pairs of words. Look up their meanings in the dictionary to make sure you understand the differences between them.

aisle   and **isle**
altar   and **alter**
bare   and **bear**
boar   and **bore**
coarse and **course**
doe   and **dough**
hoarse and **horse**
pane   and **pain**
way   and **weigh**

Here are three more pairs of words that are often confused. When you have looked the words up in the dictionary and are quite sure that you understand their meanings, write a sentence for each word, using the word with its correct meaning.

advice   and **advise**
currant and **current**
their   and **there**

What do you mean - hice?

Sometimes you want to write the plural of a word. **Plural** means the way of writing a word to show that you mean more than one. Most words are easy; we just put **s** on the end:
one girl, two girls

But some words add **es** to make the plural, like this:
one bench, two benches

There are many other ways of writing plurals, but it is difficult to give useful rules. A rule that is right for one word may not be right for a very similar word. For example we write
one mouse, two mice

but if you were to write

All of these hice have got green doors.

most people would not know what you meant. What do you mean?

The Oxford Junior Dictionary does not give the plural of every word but it gives special help with those plurals that are difficult. For instance, look up the words **shelf** and **shelves**.

Here are some words that you might find difficult. They are all in the Oxford Junior Dictionary. Write out the correct plurals.
aircraft deer half knife loaf potato thief tomato witch

I thought you were wrong

19

The Oxford Junior Dictionary can help you to spell many difficult words.

Suppose you want to write 'I thought you were wrong', but you are not sure how to spell **thought**. You know that it has something to do with thinking, so you look up **think** in the Dictionary. There you will find **thought** correctly spelt and also a sentence showing how to use it.

So that you can see how this works, look up some more words like **think** and **thought**. Here are some examples:
buy and **bought**, **rise** and **rose**, **sink**, **sank** and **sunk**.

1 Using the Dictionary, make up four sentences: one using the word **ride**, the second using the word **ridden**, the third **rode** and the fourth **riding**.

2 Using the Dictionary, make up two sentences, one using **teach** the other using **taught**.

3 Using the Dictionary, make up four sentences: the first using the word **take**, the second **took**, the third **taken**, and the fourth **taking**.

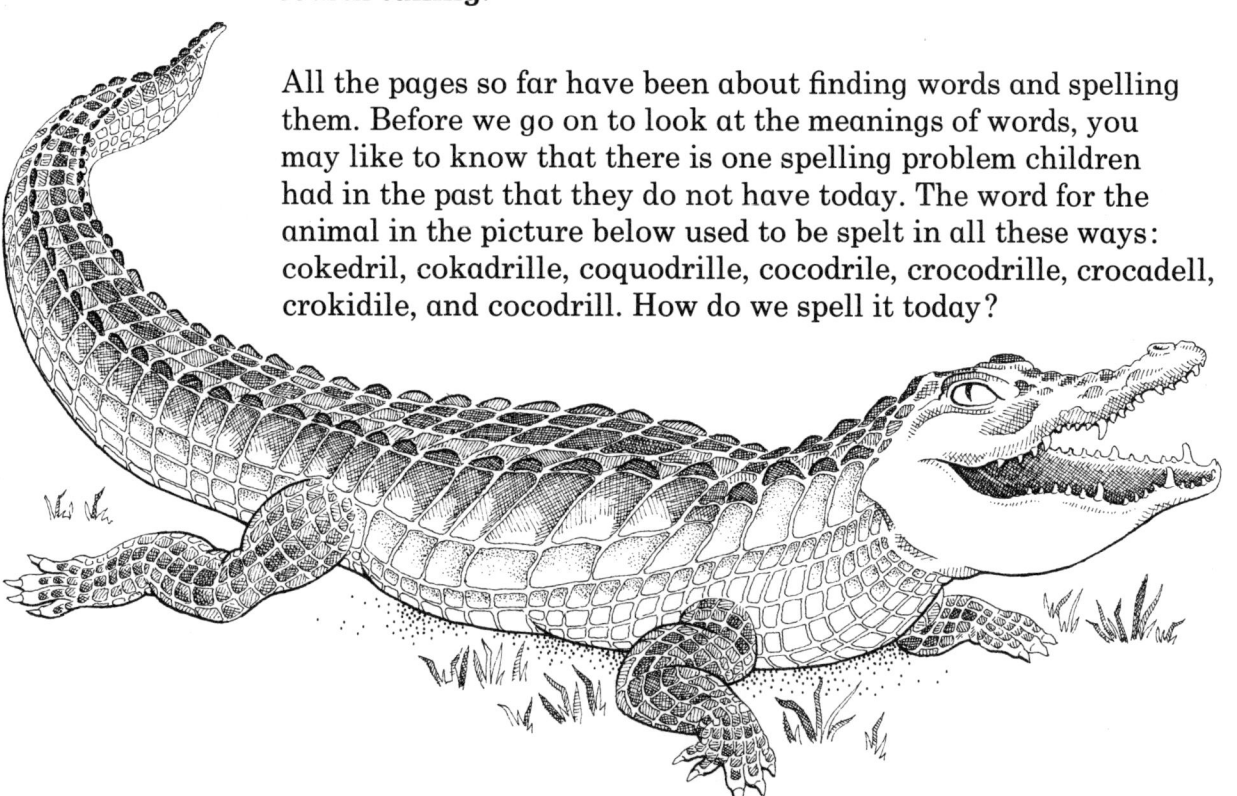

All the pages so far have been about finding words and spelling them. Before we go on to look at the meanings of words, you may like to know that there is one spelling problem children had in the past that they do not have today. The word for the animal in the picture below used to be spelt in all these ways: cokedril, cokadrille, coquodrille, cocodrile, crocodrille, crocadell, crokidile, and cocodrill. How do we spell it today?

Meanings and definitions

There are two main reasons why people look in a dictionary. The first is to find out how to spell a word. The second is to find out what a word means. So far we have been looking at the spelling of words. Now we are going to look at their meanings.
Meanings are often called **definitions** because their job is to make it quite clear or definite what the word means.

The first thing to notice is that some words have more than one meaning. Look up the word **bolt**, for example. You will see that it has four different meanings, and you will also see that each meaning is numbered, from 1 to 4.

Now look up the word **bow**. It is printed twice, like this:
bow[1]
bow[2]
The little numbers show that although these two words are spelt the same, in other ways they are different from each other. Not only do they have different meanings but they are spoken differently. The number is not part of the word and you do not include it when you are writing. **Minute**, **present**, and **read** are three more words like **bow**. Look these up too.

As well as telling you the meaning of a word, the Dictionary helps you with words that are difficult to say, like this:
bouquet (*say* boo-kay)

Finally, it is sometimes very helpful to see the word used in a sentence. When this is done in the Dictionary, it is put at the end of the definition and printed in italics, like this:
perhaps possibly
  Perhaps it will rain tomorrow.

Which way to the balcony?

All the words you have to look up for the questions on this page begin with one of the first five letters of the alphabet.

1. What sort of ending is **abrupt**?
2. What happens at an **auction**?
3. If you **adore** something, how do you feel about it?
4. What do you do when you **apologize**?
5. Would you find a **balcony** upstairs or downstairs?
6. How many balls are used in the game of **billiards**?
7. What is a **buoy** used for?
8. Which berries are found on **brambles**?
9. How fast is a **canter**?
10. What does **chrome** or **chromium** look like?
11. When you **claim** something, what do you do?
12. What is **cement** made of?
13. What kind of ship is a **destroyer**?
14. What would you do with a **divan**?
15. What is a **dome** shaped like?
16. 'I got **drenched**,' said Andrew. What did he mean?
17. What happens at an **eclipse**?
18. If you are **embarking**, are you at the beginning or the end of a voyage?
19. If someone **exaggerates**, is he telling the truth?
20. If you **extinguish** a fire, what do you do to it?

Is a crocodile a moving staircase?

When a dictionary is written, the writers have to be careful not to get the definitions muddled up, or something like this might happen:

cake something very powerful that is used for blowing things up.

dentist a large animal that lives in rivers in some hot countries. It has short legs, a long body, and sharp teeth.

bulldozer a woman who is a ballet dancer.

ankle an insect that makes a shrill sound by rubbing one leg against a wing.

escalator someone whose job is to look after teeth.

dynamite a food made with flour, butter, eggs and sugar.

ballerina a heavy machine for clearing land.

crocodile a moving staircase.

attic the thin part of the leg where it is joined to the foot.

grasshopper a room or rooms inside the roof of a house.

Use your dictionary to help you sort these out.

When you have done that, you can make up some of your own. If you write each word and definition out on a separate piece of paper and then cut off the word from the definition, you can have a game like the **Sorting Race** on page 5 of this book and see who is the first to put the right definitions to the right words.

Forts and fritters

The words you have to look up on this page begin with one of the letters from **f** to **p**.

1. What is the temperature of boiling water in **Fahrenheit**?
2. Is a **fortress** bigger or smaller than a **fort**?
3. How do you make **fritters**?
4. What does the force of **gravity** do?
5. What is the date of **Hallowe'en**?
6. What kind of line is **horizontal**?
7. What do you do if you **insult** someone?
8. What does a **joiner** do?
9. There are two meanings for the word **kiosk**. One of them is 'a telephone box'. What is the other?
10. A **launch** is a kind of boat. How is it moved along—by oars, by a sail, or by an engine?
11. What does a **licence** say?
12. What is **lint** used for?
13. What are **meringues** made of?
14. What sort of things are made in a **mint**?
15. Where might you be if you saw a **mirage**?
16. What do the **nerves** do in the body?
17. With what part of your body would you notice an **odour**—your eyes, your nose, or your ears?
18. What does an **optician** do?
19. How does a **pedestrian** get from one place to another?
20. If you **postpone** something, does that mean you send it through the post, or do it quickly, or put it off until later?

Policemen, penguins and plumbers

Here are the names of several different kinds of living creatures, with their definitions. The definitions have got attached to the wrong words. Can you sort them out?

penguin	a small pale brown animal with long back legs and very soft fur.
weasel	a sea-creature that lives inside a pair of shells.
spider	someone who puts in and mends taps and water pipes.
policeman	a kind of dog with curly hair, often cut short on some parts of its body.
plumber	a small sea fish.
leopard	a sea-creature with a shell and a long tail.
oyster	a small, furry animal with a long body. It kills and eats mice, rats, and rabbits.
poodle	a sea bird that cannot fly and uses its short, stiff wings for swimming.
sardine	a very tall African animal with a very long neck.
gerbil	a man whose job is to catch criminals and make sure the law is kept.
giraffe	a bird with large eyes that hunts smaller animals at night.
lobster	a big wild cat found in Asia and Africa. It has yellow fur with black spots on it.
owl	a small creature with eight legs that sometimes weaves webs to catch insects.

Gunpowder, treason and plot

The words you have to look up on this page begin with letters from **q** to the end of the alphabet.

1. What do people get from a **quarry**?
2. 'There's lots of lemonade!' said John. Was he talking about the **quantity** or the **quality**?
3. Where in a house would you find the **rafters**?
4. Find a word beginning with **h** that means nearly the same as **ravenous**.
5. What goes inside a **scabbard**?
6. What kind of person is a **snob**?
7. What is a **splint** used for?
8. Simon **strolled** down the road. Was he in a hurry?
9. What is **tar** made from?
10. *Remember, remember, the fifth of November,
    Gunpowder, treason, and plot.*
    What does **treason** mean?
11. What kind of engine is a **turbine**?
12. What do the people in a **union** do?
13. Is the room you are in now **vacant**?
14. There are two kinds of **wax**. What is the difference between them?
15. What is **willow** wood used for?
16. What does a **valve** in a machine do?
17. What does a **terrapin** look like?
18. What is the difference between **style** and a **stile**?
19. What happens in a **revolution**?
20. Where does a **quill** come from?

Spaghetti Junction

This is a word maze. You have to find your way from **START** at the bottom to the space at the top marked **FINISH**. When you get to a junction like this:

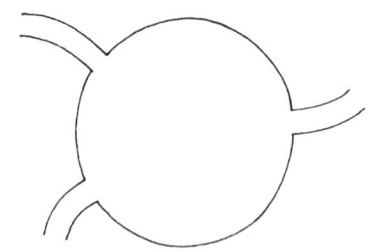

you will find a picture and two words. One of the words is the right name of the thing in the picture, and the other word is wrong. If you follow the road by the right word, it will lead you to another junction, like this:

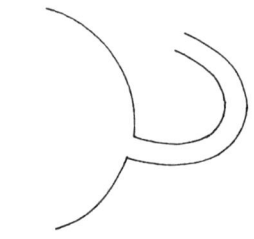

But if you choose the wrong word, it will lead you to a dead end like this:

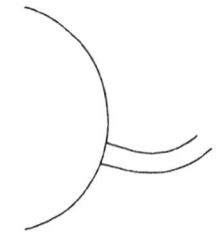

Sometimes the road will come to a bridge, like this:

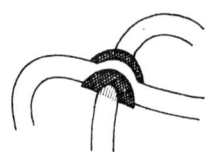

You can go over or under a bridge, but you must not go through a dead end. You can only finish the maze by choosing the right word at each of the junctions.

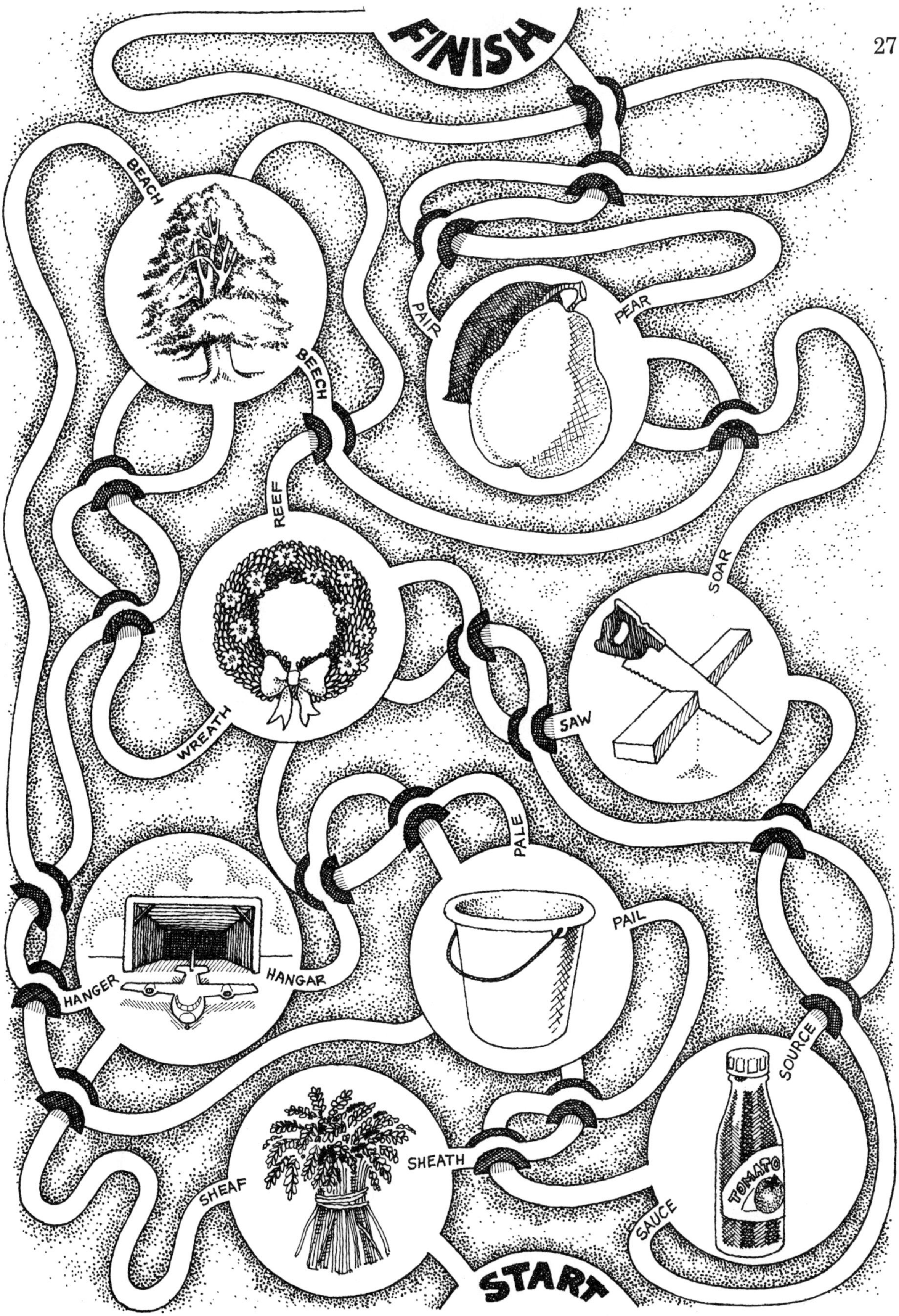
FINISH
BEACH
BEECH
PAIR
PEAR
REEF
WREATH
SOAR
SAW
PALE
PAIL
HANGER
HANGAR
SOURCE
SAUCE
SHEATH
SHEAF
TOMATO
START

Another Maze

This is like **Spaghetti Junction**, except that it is more complicated.

The rules are the same. A wrong word leads to a dead end, and a right word leads to another junction.

This time the roads loop as well, like this:

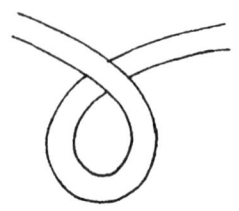

And sometimes other roads go in and out of the loops like this:

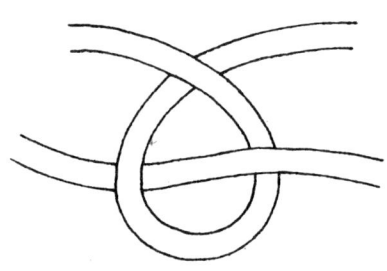

But you keep following the road you are on until it comes to a dead end or another junction.

29

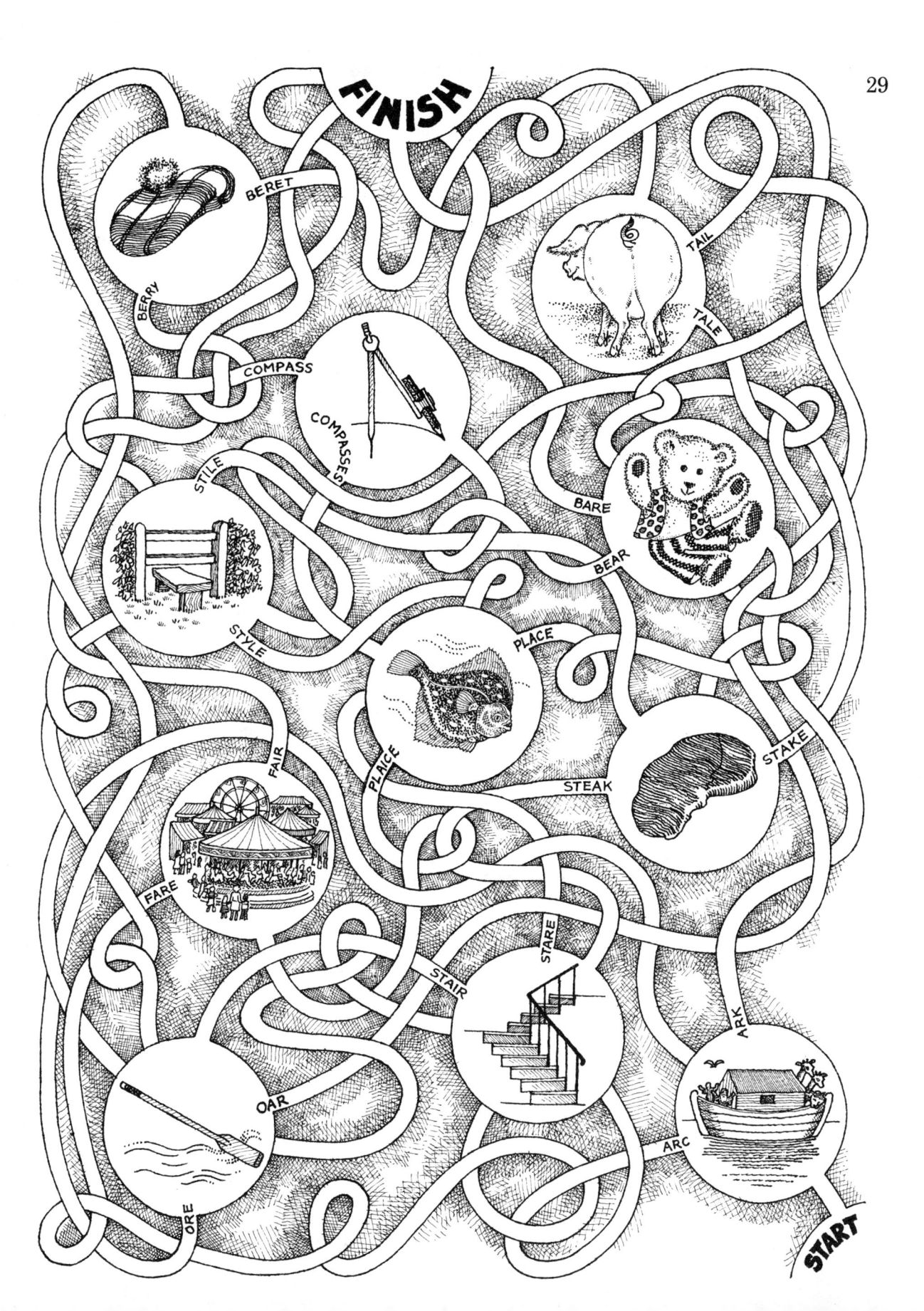

Round the Houses

A game for two or more players

What you have to do is collect the letters needed to make a six-letter word, and then take them to **HOME**.

You collect them by visiting each letter in turn with your counter, according to the throw of a dice.

You start from any of the three entrances. Take turns to throw the dice, and move your counter the number of spaces shown on the dice. You will find if you look carefully that you can get to a letter with your first throw, no matter what number comes up. That letter will be the first letter of your word.

Use the dictionary to find a six-letter word beginning with your letter, and then take turns to throw the dice and move around the board, collecting the other letters in the right order until you have the whole word. When you have done that, move your counter to **HOME**. You must throw the exact number to get there.

When you collect a letter, you must throw the exact number to get it. If you land in the space with the entrance to the letter you want, move your counter on to the letter itself and write the letter down before you throw again.

If you throw a number that is bigger than the one you need, you can keep going round and round the letter until you throw the right number to go in and collect it.

If you choose a word like **asleep**, with a letter repeated in it, land on the space to collect the first **e** and then come out and move your counter all the way around the letter before you can collect it for the second time.

The first person to go to **HOME** with all his letters is the winner.

HOME

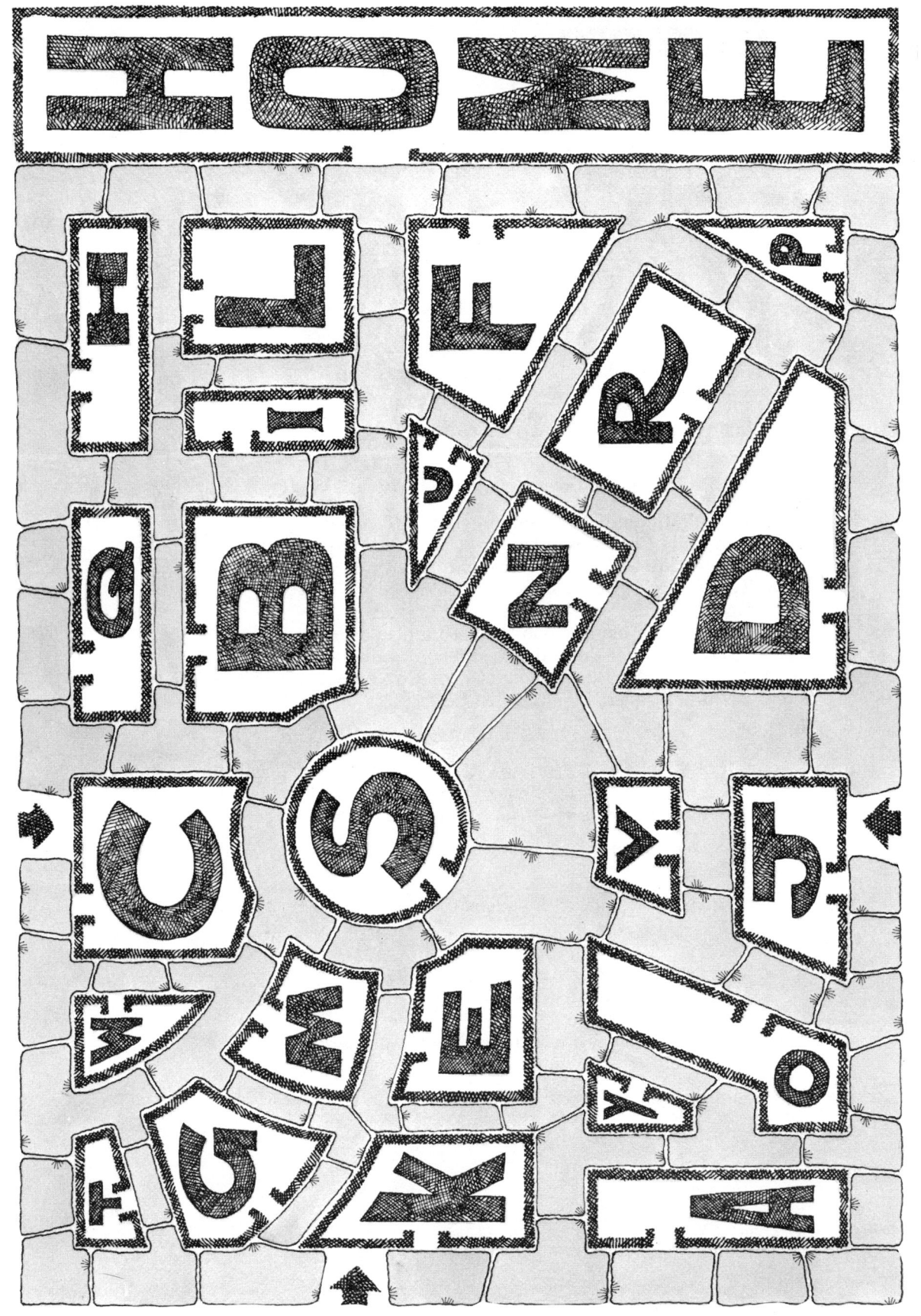

Answers

Page 2 1. ABCDEFGH 2. NOPQRSTU 3. CEFHIJK 4. BFGIJMS 5. BEJKOPQUVX

Page 3 1. air brave cabbage deceive elephant
2. Yes
3. boat funny goat monkey potato try whistle
4. Brian Helen Jenny Karen Nigel Susan Timothy
5. beans carrots eggs fish leeks mushrooms onions potatoes spinach turnips. Eggs and fish are not vegetables.

Page 4 First words: 1. baby 2. cab 3. dachshund 4. gabble 5. jab 6. kaleidoscope 7. label 8. mac 9. rabbit 10. tabby
Last words: 1. axle 2. buzz 3. cypress 4. wrung 5. just 6. quiz 7. mystery 8. hyphen 9. lying 10. tyre

Page 6 1. talented teenager thrills tired toddlers
2. Jenny Maxwell, Gary Merton, Alison Milton, Tony Moore, Carol Muncaster
3. sail sea shipwreck signal skipper submarine

Page 7 rocket submarine octopus koala bear catapult newt

Page 8 1. **Linda's Lucky Christmas** by Sally Bradshaw
The Pony Club Adventure by Caroline Brenton
Expedition to Planet X by John Bright
The White Tiger by Kevin Brown
Goals! Goals! Goals! by Andrew Bryson
2. dock dolphin domino donkey doodle doubt dove
3. decay deceit decimal declare decorate decrease
4. Alison Crabbe, David Craddock, Andrew Craig, Nigel Cramer, Karen Crane, Lorraine Craven, Simon Crawford

Page 9 helicopter penguin vulture tambourine fern penknife

Page 10 1. Turks 2. Saudis 3. Spaniard 4. the Dutch 5. a European 6. Cypriots 7. The Vietnamese 8. the Swiss 9. Greeks 10. the Portuguese 11. Afghans 12. Lapland 13. Finland 14. Danes 15. the Burmese

Page 11 1. octagon 2. heptagon 3. sphere 4. six 5. six 6. twelve 7. six 8. cylinder

Page 12 1. photograph 2. guitar 3. physical 4. guess, guinea, guilty 5. Guide

Page 13 1. gentle, giraffe, gingerbread 2. gnawing 3. knocked 4. genuine 5. knob

Page 14 1. There was a huge centipede on the salad.
2. My favourite sport is wrestling.
3. Sometimes I cycle to school.
4. I wrote a sentence about a wreck but it was wrong.
5. I like sugar and milk on my cereal.

Page 15 1. choir, Christmas 2. chrysalis 3. chauffeur 4. hours 5. chorus

Page 18 aircraft deer halves knives loaves potatoes tomatoes thieves witches